FEB - - 2015

# Down in the DEEP, DEEP OCEAN!

Rourke Publishing LLC
Vero Beach, Florida 32964

Jo Cleland

© 2009 Rourke Publishing LLC

All rights reserved. No part of this book may be reproduced or utilized in any form or by any means, electronic or mechanical including photocopying, recording, or by any information storage and retrieval system without permission in writing from the publisher.

www.rourkepublishing.com

PHOTO CREDITS: © Damon Taylor: All Illustrations; © mphotoi, © Rick Miller: Title Page; © Sebastian Meckelmann: page 3; 22; © Jean-Yves Benedeyt: page 5, 19, 22, 23; © Digital Vision: page 7; © Adam White: page 9; © Joe Belanger: page 11; © fmg1308: page 13; © Dan Schmitt: page 15, 23; © Jeffery Zavitski: page 17; © Dennis Sabo: page 21

Editor: Jeanne Sturm

Cover design by: Heather Botto

Interior design by: Renee Brady

**Library of Congress Cataloging-in-Publication Data**

Cleland, Joann.
 Down in the deep, deep ocean! / Jo Cleland.
    p. cm. -- (My first science library)
  ISBN 978-1-60472-534-6
 1. Marine animals--Juvenile literature. I. Title.
  QL122.2.C58 2009b
  591.77--dc22
                                                    2008027356

Printed in the USA

CG/CG

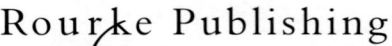

www.rourkepublishing.com – rourke@rourkepublishing.com
Post Office Box 3328, Vero Beach, FL 32964

What lives down in the deep, deep ocean?

"I live down in the deep, deep ocean," squawks the playful penguin.

5

"I live down in the deep, deep ocean," sighs the shiny hammerhead shark.

"We live down in the deep, deep ocean," squeak the dancing dolphins.

"I live down in the deep, deep ocean," whispers the silent starfish.

"I live down in the deep, deep ocean," snarls the slithery eel.

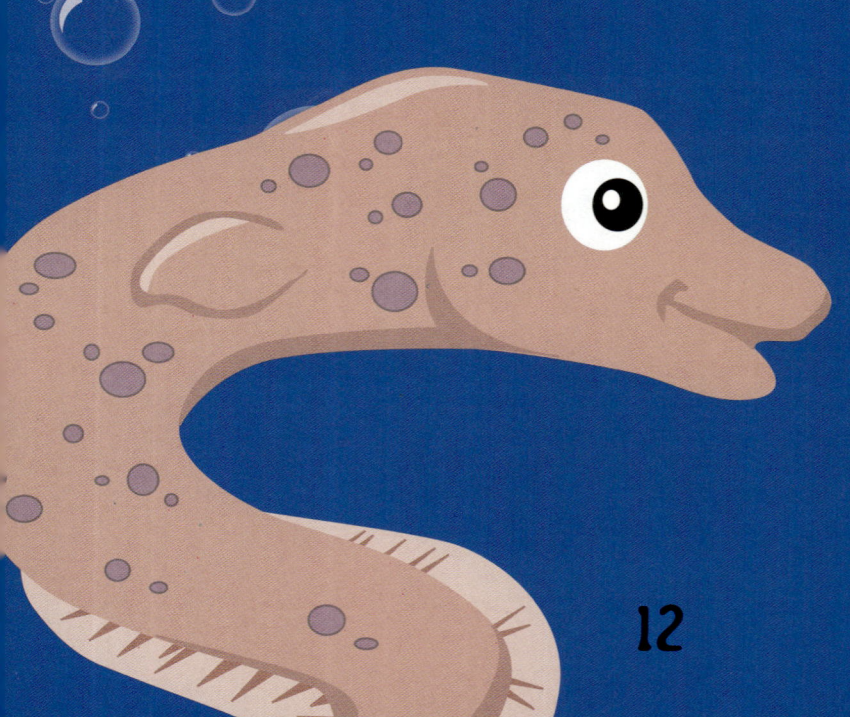

"I live down in the deep, deep ocean," slurps the slimy squid.

"I live down in the deep, deep ocean," sings the whistling Beluga whale.

17

"We live down in the deep, deep ocean," bubble the curly coral reefs.

"I don't live in the deep, deep ocean," says the deep-sea diver. "But I like to go down there to visit all my animal friends."

# Glossary

coral reefs (KOR-uhl REEFZ): A coral reef is a pile of bones left behind when corals (little sea animals) die. Many species of fish find protection and shelter in coral reefs. Coral reefs also protect coastlines from strong currents and waves.

ocean (OH-shuhn): An ocean is a large body of salt water. Oceans cover about 71 percent of the Earth's surface.

**penguin** (PEN-gwin): Penguins are birds that spend much of their lives swimming in icy cold waters. Penguins eat fish, squid, and other food from the sea. A layer of fat, called blubber, and fluffy feathers, called down, help penguins stay warm.

**squid** (SKWID): A squid is a sea creature that looks something like a little octopus. It uses its tentacles (arms) to catch food.

# Index

coral reefs     18, 19
deep-sea diver     20, 21
dolphins     8, 9
eel     12, 13
penguin     4, 5
shark     6, 7
squid     14, 15
starfish     10, 11
whale     16, 17

## Further Reading

Raffi. *Baby Beluga*. Crown Publishers, 1990.
Whitehouse, Patty. *Living in an Ocean*. Rourke, 2007.
Windsor, Jo. *Big Animals in the Sea*. Rigby, 1999.

## Websites

www.hello-world.com/children/English/ocean.php
www.kllynch2000.com/Ocean.html
www.atozkidsstuff.com/ocean.html
www.dltk-kids.com/animals/ocean.html

## About the Author

Jo Cleland loves to write books, compose songs, and make games. She loves to read, sing, and play games with children.